IT'S TIME TO EAT PAPAYAS

It's Time to Eat PAPAYAS

Walter the Educator

Silent King Books
A WhichHead Entertainment Imprint

Copyright © 2024 by Walter the Educator

All rights reserved. No part of this book may be reproduced in any manner whatsoever without written per- mission except in the case of brief quotations embodied in critical articles and reviews.

First Printing, 2024

Disclaimer

This book is a literary work; the story is not about specific persons, locations, situations, and/or circumstances unless mentioned in a historical context. Any resemblance to real persons, locations, situations, and/or circumstances is coincidental. This book is for entertainment and informational purposes only. The author and publisher offer this information without warranties expressed or implied. No matter the grounds, neither the author nor the publisher will be accountable for any losses, injuries, or other damages caused by the reader's use of this book. The use of this book acknowledges an understanding and acceptance of this disclaimer.

It's Time to Eat PAPAYAS is a collectible early learning book by Walter the Educator suitable for all ages belonging to Walter the Educator's Time to Eat Book Series. Collect more books at WaltertheEducator.com

USE THE EXTRA SPACE TO TAKE NOTES AND DOCUMENT YOUR MEMORIES

PAPAYAS

The sun is warm, the sky is bright,

It's Time to Eat
Papayas

It's time for a treat, a fruity delight.

Green on the outside, orange inside,

Papayas are here, let's open them wide!

Long and smooth, they feel so neat,

Filled with goodness, juicy and sweet.

Cut them open, take a look,

Tiny black seeds like dots in a book.

Scoop the seeds, then take a bite,

The flavor's soft and feels so right.

It's mellow, fruity, mild, and true,

Papayas are good for me and you!

"Add some lime!" my sister cheers,

A sprinkle of juice, and taste appears.

The tangy twist, the citrus zest,

Makes papayas taste their best.

It's Time to Eat
Papayas

In smoothies, salads, or just plain,

Papayas shine again and again.

Blend them up, so creamy and fine,

A tropical drink that feels divine.

"Did you know?" says Grandpa, wise,

"Papayas are healthy, a wonderful prize!

They help you grow, they're good for your tummy,

And best of all, they're super yummy!"

Birds and bees love them too,

A fruit for all in skies so blue.

In every garden, near and far,

Papayas are nature's shining star.

"Can we plant the seeds?" I ask with glee,

"To grow a papaya tree for me!"

Dig a hole and water each day,

It's Time to Eat
Papayas

Soon green leaves will come our way.

The season's here, it won't last long,

Papayas sing their tropical song.

Pick them ripe, don't let them wait,

A fruit this good is truly great!

So grab a papaya, slice it wide,

And share it with loved ones by your side.

A fruit so special, soft, and sweet,

It's Time to Eat
Papayas

Hooray for papayas, a joy to eat!

ABOUT THE CREATOR

Walter the Educator is one of the pseudonyms for Walter Anderson. Formally educated in Chemistry, Business, and Education, he is an educator, an author, a diverse entrepreneur, and he is the son of a disabled war veteran. "Walter the Educator" shares his time between educating and creating. He holds interests and owns several creative projects that entertain, enlighten, enhance, and educate, hoping to inspire and motivate you. Follow, find new works, and stay up to date with Walter the Educator™

at WaltertheEducator.com

www.ingramcontent.com/pod-product-compliance
Lightning Source LLC
LaVergne TN
LVHW052013060526
838201LV00059B/4016